T0077944

YOGA BECAUSE

The Rise Into My Yogic Journey

GINGER HUNT

BALBOA.PRESS

A DIVISION OF HAY HOUSE

Balboa Press books may be ordered through booksellers or by contacting:

Balboa Press
A Division of Hay House
1663 Liberty Drive
Bloomington, IN 47403
www.balboapress.com
844-682-1282

Print information available on the last page.

ISBN: 978-1-9822-6697-4 (sc)
ISBN: 978-1-9822-6698-1 (e)

Balboa Press rev. date: 04/16/2021

This is dedicated to my children because I want to gift them a positive focus and tools in their life for self-love and healing. From the things that I have learned from and that I do in my daily life for self-love and healing.

I dedicate this to all the real life angels in my life who have crossed paths with me through the years to share their love, compassion, empathy and have empowered me along the way.

And I dedicate this also to the ones who have made it difficult on me, who have defied me, who have not embraced me and who have not loved me. It is all a gift too! And they have taught me many different things. All of these things have empowered me in ways to the act of self-love and healing for myself.

*I'm grateful for all my life experiences
and what they have taught me.*

Because why not turn inward and adjust the frequency of self-love and healing. That's what I did. Hence the rise into my yogic journey. I'll share the different limbs of yoga which gave me ease in my daily life. The things that I do to walk a healthier walk. I'll share with you in a format that's easy to read and each … because… can be explored to the fullest by yourself. It's giving you short little but big actions on the act of self-love and healing. It's not perfectly detailed for the reasons of it being simpler and conversational. So it's a light hearted read to take with you and be explored on the level you would like to explore it.

Because if I overthink this or try to perfect it I may lose the joy. It's writing this book with joy and intent to help give you insight of the process. Perfection is not my goal and this brings me to writing this in my laid-back style. The words describe how I choose to live and which evolved to more self love and healing.

Because healing has been my focus for myself. It's self realizations for me as I became a Certified Practical Yoga Instructor Training and then Yogafit Teacher Training Yogafit For Warriors. I want to enlighten others to knowing how all of the things that we do, do affect the body. I want to bring awareness that we have tools. I want to bring awareness of the control we have in our life and with our health too. So then we can all make the best decision for ourselves. What we choose today affects tomorrow.

Self realization

Because at an early age I discovered all energy frequencies that people emit. And as an adult I've come to accept all the different energy frequencies people have. After reflecting I've known which frequencies I desired to be functioning in amongst my life. I chose to reflect on what frequencies I wanted to be surrounded by. A mixture of the energies occurs without doubt but again I bring myself back to awareness of which energy is around, I accept it fully and then I steer myself to be where I want to function. I am carefully attuned to the energy frequencies surrounding myself. I accept what is and in turn focus on my energy and protecting my energy too.

Because I've gifted myself by exploring the energy frequency I thrive in and I focus on this. I also am driven to connect with ones of the like. And it literally feeds my body and my mind to an elevated state. Which entails gives way to homeostasis, repair and self regulation in my body. I accept the different energy frequencies of people but I'm aware which ones I thrive within. This can mean at times being solo so that I am still thriving in this state.

I choose to be mindful of the energy that I thrive in.

Because I got to the point in my life where I discovered
another job title or another degree isn't the answer
to more self love and healing. Instead of getting
distracted by trying to better myself in that way I
chose to sit still in all the feelings and accept all of the
actualization of what is…. I chose to reflect instead of
deflect. Reflect on my best energy frequency and what
brings me to that best energy that I desire to be in.
And this is where I spend my time. At this University
discovering and living with intent of self love and
healing to the degree of my best version of myself.

Because I chose throughout my days to discover inner peace and define what that looks like. And some of those days may not be a beach walk and toes in the sand kind of day. It may be snow packed and cold. The sun does shine in all of these places. I choose to be in the sun wherever I am. And bring the "beach" to me. The "beach" is an inner stillness kind of feeling in the sunshine. It's sitting in the sun in the present moment and embracing life down to the cellular level. I explored all the ways I can sit in the sun comfortably in the winter time. The sunroof in my vehicle allowed me to do just this many days. Opening a window in the house and getting sunshine coming through that window. And/or also finding a wind protected area outside in the sun on a decent day. I embraced bringing the "beach" to myself.

I focus on that inner stillness that "the beach" brings me.

Because I attuned to the mind and body connection which is a huge key to health. No matter what stage of health we are in we can reassess our life and bring it to a level of self regulation. I regrouped in my life and came back to the mind–body connection being my focus.

Because I matter in this equation. My body is my vessel
in the here and now. I did find my way to my best self.
I explored what my best self looks like. My mind and
body connection is thriving in this best self state and
even down to the cellular level. I know that less energy
exerted as a whole causes my body to have more energy
for repair for homeostasis, self-regulation and repair.
With this limb of yoga, Yama, mindfulness gives way
to regulated health, healing and longevity in my body.

Because slowing down and being aware of the breath rate. Pranayama, a limb of yoga, brings so much health, healing and repair to the body. Our breathing shows us what functioning actually looks like and down to the cellular level. It's a reflection if we are functioning in fight or flight or a parasympathetic nervous system.
I am mindful of this every second. I slow my breath often; daily, hourly, and upon minutes at times. I slow my breath down and control the pattern as well. I focus on a breathing pattern of four breaths in pause and four breaths out. And if I'm sitting or laying I can focus on slowing it down even more to 6–8 second count breaths in and pause slowly releasing 6–8 count breaths out. Being aware of the breath patterns, controlling the breathing and slowing it down in turn slows the heart rate down and gives us more ease and life. Our heart beating pumping every second of every day of our life gives us a huge awareness of being mindful of our breathing rate and our heart rate. We can give ourselves more health and longevity by slowing our breathe down and our heart rate comes down naturally by doing this.

Because if a dreadlock or two or three makes
you feel good- Just do it. If coloring your hair,
braiding your hair, a ball cap or space buns makes
you feel good. Do it. I did! I had fun getting
creative with my hair which made me happy.

Because if a tattoo gives you an energy frequency, joy
or peace in your mind and body – just do it. I did!

Because my voice in my head guides me to this higher
energy frequency. I am mindful of this energy frequency
that I carry in my mind. So I feed and I nurture
the voice in my head to this elevated frequency.

Because why not be present in the five senses. It
actually keeps you in the now. Savor the senses you
love; if it's the food on your tastebuds, the aroma,
the visuals, the sounds or the touch. I always bring
my attention and focus to the senses and savor the
ones I love. And on the flip side of this I explore the
limb of yoga, Pratyahara, which is the practice of
withdrawing the senses from the outer world. Through
this withdrawal, I heighten my inner awareness.

Because I choose to focus on love. It's the state of peace. I let go of all expectations. Love is the only reality and at the heart of creativity. It's the mindful state that gives way to self repair, regulation and homeostasis in the body.

Choose to focus on Love!

Because every day throughout the day the energy
frequency I carry radiates around me. I choose to
smile more, to uplift another and to carry this vibe so
it radiates to another. I know it radiates internally and
affects my mind and body connection. I practice the
act of this and focus on this being my neutral. I come
back to this in the ever changing of time and space.

Because I find the things that fill me up which I call lovelies. In the ever changing time and space I find the "beach", my children, the sunshine, the flowers, animals and trees! These are only some of my loves. These are some of the lovelies that fill me up.

Because music fills up my soul I find it often. And I make sure that it matches the energy frequency I desire and that it fills me up. I'm very mindful of the choice because I am feeding my mind and thus feeding my body. It could be a great 80s, rock Pop hip-hop or chill coffee house. Find it often and feed the soul! I do!

Because dancing feels good to the mind and body. I dance often. My comfort zone is to dance. I make it my comfort zone. I fill myself up with dancing. I let my body move and be free into the sound, into the beat and I let it guide my body. I feel the movement in my body freeing tension, freeing energy and I'm freer. It's a total body release. I do it to release tension in my body, release the psoas and feel the freedom of flow in my body.

Because I give love and receive love. I'm open to this process of giving love and receiving love. I allow "another" to give love to me. The actionable love and I accept and enjoy the gift of love and affection. Being aware of what this looks and feels like is a beautiful thing. It elevates me and I'm grateful for the feel good it offers. It is the state of being that offers the body healing, self regulation and repair.

Because I am elevated by all the people in my life that have gifted me love in different ways. Even though it may have been short, temporary or long ago. The genuine state of love that people have shown me is healing.

Because if I decide to go have fun and feed my soul
I'm mindful of losing some sleep. The greater good
is that I fed my soul and my body that feels good
energy. Afterwards I proceed to come back to the
resting phase and I fill myself up with the rest that I
need. Sleep is such a big factor in our life and I just
make sure I get good consistent nights sleep in general
and rest when I can if needed. I regroup back to
balance and rest as needed when an imbalance occurs.

Because if I notice I am edgy and not in my best energy
zone I attuned to what is going on and why I may be
edgy. I notice if my kids are edgy. I bring awareness
to the state of energy and assess this with them. I help
them assess why they are edgy and we go through
that check off list and figure out what they may need
to do to come back to a peaceful state of being.

Because I explore all the things that can give me health and benefits. I explore essential oils. I explore what they do in the body, the energy that they give to the body. I explore the cause-and-effect that they have on the body and I incorporate them into my life and well-being.

Because I now am aware of the connections that
I have with people and the universal lining up of
people connecting. I now see the people that I meet
as awareness. I don't see them as a means to an
end but rather I see that I should not project what
meeting another means in any way or form. I take
the stance of just letting the universal connectivity
lineup and that indeed unfolds how it's going to.
And I have peace about this awareness it offers.

Because I am aware of not fearing the good. Nothing is to fear if it's good. In the present moment of awareness and just being is a place where there is no fear. Fear is projection and ego based. If you're still to see, be aware and present you will see all you need in that state of truth. With ease it will guide you by the simple act of being present, aware and with stillness to see clearly.

Because I choose fruit and vegetables as a food option. I delight in how they were created and they were not processed. I enjoy eating them with that knowingness and health in mind. I'm totally attune to food feeding the body for energy, nutrition to the cellular level and that is the sole purpose.

Because I know if I am feeling emotional that I
need to just feel it. Feelings will come and they
will go. By sitting in the feelings it allows them
to be felt. And then to be released as needed.
And going forward will be with more ease.

Because by being aware of the pain body that exists from life experiences and not attaching it forward in the future with no reason to. I am so much freer by being aware of this and not doing this. And when another has the pain body I'm aware and not attached to theirs. I'm staying in consciousness and aware the other is in unconscious pain. By being aware of this truth it sets us free.

Because I'm mindful of the path of least resistance gives more ease. Fighting energy is exerting energy. I look at the body as a pool of energy. I am mindful of all this energy as a whole. I am aware of the cause and effect of what it takes to keep energy at a steady level versus the exertion of replacing the energy in the body.

Because I know and I'm aware of the difference between hard and easy. Why choose hard!?! It doesn't have to be hard to find success. Success does come with a level of hard but find ease within the levels. Going with the current and the flow instead of fighting it brings ease into mind and the body.

Because I focus on the calm centeredness of myself.
I choose to focus on this flow of energy.
It gives way to this present moment. It offers a way to
grow everyday and to see new opportunities amidst.
Creating this state of mind can be done at any time. I
am mindful when I need to do a reset. I reflect if I am
the person I want to be!?! And knowing when I am the
person I want to be that this is where the best flow is.

Focusing on the calm centeredness of myself.

Because If there are conditions or conditioned people that are around me that I'm aware of this. I reposition myself physically and/or mentally where I need to be according to this. It might mean going solo to the dance and/or finding new people to be surrounded with. I've learned if I'm waiting for the right people to accompany me then I'll be waiting for a while or perhaps miss my enjoyment. When what I desire to do isn't going to occur I decide to go solo. And in this process- guess what? I found people to connect with in doing this. Instead of missing out I am able to partake and connect potentially with others which has been such a beautiful gift.

I focus on my creative energy as that is a thriving place to be. Creativity is the highest place we can be in our state of being. Creativity is effortless energy that renews us to a lighter being.

Because I focus on getting unstuck as a whole, whatever
that may be. I'm present and aware to see what stuck
looks like and how to evolve out of it. If it's a PTSD
nightmare; I awakened to stop the story created and put a
halt to it. I made choices to get counsel with the process.
I learned how to free the mind from having them. I
released them by the process of IRT(image rehearsal
therapy) and changing the end story by becoming alert
and aware in the nightmare and changing the end
story to a beautiful end. I've been reprogramming my
mind with guided meditations. And I'm able to say I no
longer have those PTSD nightmares. I closed the gap for
change and got out of old patterns. I'm set free to move
forward without these limits. The past conditioning
no longer serves me. Being stuck isn't permanent.
I always explore my options when I feel stuck. It is
changeable. Life flows easily when we are unstuck.

Because I explore and use all my resources
for the limitless potential awaiting me.
I am fulfilled when I can be who I was meant to
be. The purest of flow is when who I was meant
to be meets with my limitless possibilities.

Because I allow myself to feel the complaint and
then choose to self regulate and let go. I understand
the simple cause and effect type response in
the body. I don't stay in complaining I come
back to "my Beach" and "my sunshine".

Because chaos can create beautiful things but I'm also mindful of the chaos. I steer away from the chaos that results in hindering or not bringing good results.

Because a calm country drive brings peace to a destiny.
Or a city stressed drive brings me to a calm beachy
destination. I stay focused on the calm destiny.

Because when I sit for extended periods I know that my muscles in my body get tight. Therefore I move my hips east to west and my spinal column east to west with ease to get movement in my spinal column. I do pelvic tilt's right where I'm at if it's in the car seat or in a chair. These can be done anywhere. I'm very mindful of taking care of my body and getting a simple release in my body. Not a day goes by where I don't incorporate a limb of yoga, Niyama, mindful observations of my poses or postures. I'm a practicing Yogi for life.

Because I'm choosing to be mindful of my career and my work day and attuned to my mind body connection. My breathing, my muscle tension, and my heart rate pulse tells me if I'm doing right by myself. The monetary exchange for health awareness is so important to assess. Be aware of the external asset abundance versus internal abundance ratio. Real abundance is the reflection of the joyful energetic body. Abundance comes from within the self and our thoughts, intention, the attention and our expectations indeed shape these thoughts.

Because being in nature connects to the air of the universe. I breathe it in mindfully. It shows me how I exist in this universe. It teaches me so much. It teaches me about energy, universal intelligence and information amidst too.

Being present in the moment.

Because when I walk erect with intent it feels good.
I have intention within my body, my walk and
my balance. I may even alter my walk to get more
movement in areas in my body. I may move my
hips, or open my chest more when I walk because it
feels good. I strive to just feel good in my body!

Because embracing the unknown and accepting unknowns is also bringing me peace to my mind and my body. It's a known fact that unknowns occur anyways. So I remind myself this often.

Because slowing myself down and healing looks
different than just doing fitness exercise. There is
so much healing in slowing my pace. Practicing a
limb of Yoga, Asana, has shown me how to slow my
pace. It's taught me the most minute movement of
the body has a benefit. I'm making sure I'm getting
out of auto pilot body movements and auto pilot
exercising. I'm being mindful of these movements
and reaping the benefits of slowing down. It's about
reprogramming my movements and muscles to a state
before auto pilot. It's healing in so many ways.

Because I choose to not stay in collective unconsciousness of what others have taught me. I'm not seeking others and their portrayals of how they think life is supposed to be. I'm aware of this freedom in the consciousness and what this brings to me. It sets me free.

Because I'm choosing to detach from external messages
and choosing to live in pure consciousness. In this
pure consciousness I am… this whole present being
as I am…. I am…self regulating, and self evolving.
Being in the present moment is the present moment
when I stay in pure consciousness. Inturn this gives
way to pure creativity with infinite possibilities.

Because I focus on letting go of everything that does not serve me. I let go and release all negativity. When I do this I am freer and more available for the things I desire.

Because I sit still in this body and do a mental body scan. In doing this I assess my body and where there may be pain, tension or just neutral in my body. And then I focus on ease in my body with the mindfulness of what I need to change perhaps to add ease. I focus on ease in my mind and body connection. The unease tells me to assess and create ease.

Because I ask myself what am I choosing !?!
What new choices can I make to achieve my
new goals!?! I invite unlimited choices and I
ask for unlimited abundance in my life.

Because I don't compare myself to others. I stay out of that zone. I look inside myself for fulfillment. I can access this internal fulfillment at any time. I stay focused on everything that I desire is within me.

Staying in my zone.

Because I know what I am focusing on is actually what I am manifesting. If it's this writing this book, health, love, peace, joy or … I am creating what I'm focusing on.

Because when I sing it triggers the parasympathetic
nervous system response. I am stimulating the
Vagus nerve with the singing vibrations and
it brings calmness to the body. I sing often
to trigger this response in my body.

Because I'm focused on vibrational subtle sounds that heal The body. Particular sounds at certain frequencies give way to lower stress, improved healing and decrease physical pain. Different sound frequencies are used to redirect your brain waves and promote physical healing. In the brain all the neurons get stimulated at different frequencies based on the data. The neurons in the brain get stimulated from things around us. And the vibrations are interacting with every single cell in our bodies.

Because I've explored the "who am I?" The basics of just "I am"....Not the labels, not the ego, not the conditioned self, not titles or careers. I just am ....Literally that I just am. I am enough just in the state of I am and I am whole just as I am. Without absolutely anything else more than just I am. I am free to be just this. I am... Because I know; I am whole as I am. I am the direct healer of my body and the healed of my body as well.

Because I chose to chant, I hum, and I create a vibration sound that stimulates the Vagus nerve. By stimulating the Vagus nerve I give way to lowered stress, relaxation and self-regulation in my nervous system. Also I use subtle humming as a tool to help get rid of migraines or headaches too. When I had Covid I used this throughout the days to combat the headaches. That helped me alleviate the headaches I had with Covid.

Because I am enlightened in awareness of truth
and pain bodies do exist. I examine myself and
others and don't choose to stay in this suffering. I
hold space for the other, discern the level of space
the other has in my life and to what degree.

Because I explore western and eastern medicine and I have explored how to get release in my whole body. I've explored how to get health and self-regulation. I have done many things and many modalities to get release in my body. The majority of these modalities have been dry needling, ayurveda, surgeries, massage, acupressure, PEMF, Dhyana, a limb of yoga of focused meditation, infrared lights, tapping, cbd, hot tub, negative ion exposure, ice, heat, yoga, grounding, deep breathing, mind and body awareness, counsel for insight, and subtle body energy work. I explore integrated medicine so all combined therapies help me to get the health I desire and homeostasis. I have integrated western and eastern medicine which have helped me in more ways than I can say that it's not either or it's everything in this realm.

Because I choose to retrain my brain. Through
meditation, being aware and by releasing constructs
to set my mind free from nightmares, lessened
inflammation and less stress in the body. We can
retrain our mind and we can be set free. I'm doing the
happy dance because I did and broke these patterns.

Because I let go. I forgave all in my life for myself to set myself free. The Dis-Ease In my life was the driving force. The ease I brought to myself by forgiving is priceless. It set me free. Whatever the other person does that's their business and their work to be done. It's not my work. I am free and free of this pain and can chose the level of any other in my life. It was a choice to free me! And I'm forever grateful that I chose to set me free!

Because I have explored the trauma in my life and effects it's had emotionally and physically in my life. I have assessed the physical response that trauma has held in my body and explored all ways to get release. Through counsel I explored opening safe doors to growth, evolving through the trauma to release it, exploring my voice, and being around safe people. Psychedelics can be explored in a professional setting to help get out of ptsd type trauma and can be explored short term to release trauma. EMDR can be explored to help release trauma. Many prescriptions can be an aid short term in the process. During my journey of discovering yoga movements, completely absorbed in meditation Dharana, a limb of yoga, to quiet and calm my overthinking, sitting still and combining it with breath work have set me free. These have brought a huge amount of trauma release to my life. I'm free from it. I understand it and I did the work. I can now share how I got ease in my life!

Because I've explored my people picking skills through my life. I am very aware of who is close to me and on what level and also who is afar in my life. I'm very aware of how important having the right safe people in my life is. This indeed shapes my life in so many ways, by the success in my life and my whole body cellular health level.

Because I started living for my happiness. I
reassessed if I was living in happiness.
I stopped waiting on others to join me in the happiness
journey. I found I was always waiting on others to
enjoy life with. And I was continually waiting.
So I stopped waiting and started creating
it for me. I chose happy!

Because I choose every morning to assess what I will do to take care of myself each day. I choose throughout my day to incorporate yoga, healing, meditation, calmness, aromatherapy, calm music, breathing and choosing to be in parasympathetic mode. I reflect and act on all the things that bring me to this state of being.

Because I am scanning my body and looking for
areas that hold trauma or pain. I utilize all the
different modalities that I can do to release pain and
tightness in the muscles and body. I utilize Massage.
I bought myself a Thera gun and I also use negative
ions, infrared heating pad, Pmef, self massage, ice,
and the infrared sauna. And I'm releasing trauma
and pain in my body by attuning and practicing
yoga. I use any or all of these tools in a given day.

The warrior carrying on in the infrared sauna.

Because I focus on the small changes, baby steps and rebuilding them is timely. It's all the little steps that make the whole change occur.

Because I learned and practiced to stop thinking
and overthinking, and stop replaying negative
subconscious programs. I am taking myself out
of the mind. I am operating from awareness now.
I am able to observe my behavior and others.
I'm not functioning from the subconscious and
I'm not disempowering or self sabotaging. I'm
staying conscious and manifesting my wishes and
desires in a wonderful creative conscious state.

Because I see myself as trillions of cells functioning together. My mind reads the interpretation of the environment around me which in turn determines the composition in my blood, this chemistry and the health in my body. I know the state of being which enhances my cells, my blood to be healthy and my health in general. When our cells are healthy we are healthy. I focus on this and I am in control of this.

Because I have used the pain that I've had in my
life to come out of the very pain. I am looking
at the life lessons that each has taught me. I've
felt many pains and have come out of them. All
of these lessons are huge gifts to myself.

Because I am choosing to be in the present moment.
My past story doesn't define me. I'm aware of the past
story and I'm aware of being present in the moment.
My focus is that I can create greatness from here.
I focus on real hope, trust and
possibility and I hold onto this.

Because I choose to live in the moment and
enjoy each moment. I choose to be thankful
for these moments. And I am choosing to fully
experience life to its fullest by doing this.

Because I let go of the constructs in the mind that
were all environmentally created. The environment,
family, society, and culture are all things that
create these constructs. I'm aware of where these
constructs come from and the limitations.
I focus on literally being one with my
whole self with zero constructs.

Because I focus on existing in non-judgment non-diversion and not on "the other". I am focused on creating the energy I desire.

Because I explore all the important choices that I've made and know that good and bad comes out of all decisions. I am focusing on staying in the knowingness, and awareness to stay in ease. Upon embracing being ok with what it is and at ease in that state of being certainly makes me aware if and how I need to find ease in the situation.

Because I know how the mind works I focus on making the most of every experience and letting go of each experience to make room for the next experience. It's a skill and with no anticipation of the next experience is when the act of spontaneous thinking occurs. This is the ultimate in knowing. Joy occurs in each moment, time flies and the greatest of health occurs in the state of joy.

Because when I'm taking care of my children, working
or whatever that takes me out of the stillness in my mind.
I make sure and find a level of stillness in my mind.

Because I see the big picture of the whole year as a whole not as increments. I stop and smell the roses, I watch the first bee in the spring, I look at the spring buds, I watch the fall leaves fall, I embrace winter as it breaks the bug cycle, I embrace the calm snow falling in a muted world. I enjoy the thunderstorms that roll through. And I soak up the sunshine all year!

Because I role-play in my awareness and consciousness.
I reflect on what decision I'm contemplating
and role-play the decision. If it brings me peace
or joy or whatever it actually brings!?!

Because I bring my focus to ease just as the heart beats with ease. In a sort of choiceless awareness state of being. Flowing with the flow of ease, efficiently and not tons of thoughts. Just as the body functions so efficiently with its maximum diversity.

Because I focus on observing before I react I'm looking
at the experience and the choice because I know I
have a choice to be conscious or unconscious.
I can be an observer of the mind. I'm not
manipulating the mind but observing it. And I
keep practicing this until it's second nature.

Because I do a full body scan in stillness in my days. I feel what I need upon assessing my body. I send my body good healing energy. I may do an Epsom salt soak to calm my body and get ease with the magnesium. I spend time releasing tightness in my body. I utilize relaxation, massage, yoga, stretching, music and meditation. I am being mindful and opening up the chakras energies in my body.

Because I explore the nutrients that my body needs and the micro nutrients and if I'm getting them in the foods I'm eating. I make sure and supplement them as needed. I explore what the body needs and I'm very mindful of what I am taking in as well.

A blood draw in the lab can elaborate on some of these levels of nutrients in the blood. There are a few over the counter testing options for some as well.

Because I'm aware of my menstrual cycle and premenstrual hormone change in my energy level. I'm aware if I'm edgy, have less energy and I am not as patient. I alter the things I can to give ease to myself and others. At times I may limit myself in my doings. I give myself grace and ease during these times that I need it. For me doing this avoids unnecessary unease. I give myself more space, less doing and maybe limiting my time with others to ease frustrations. These all help add ease during the hormonal fluctuations that my pre-menstrual cycle brings on.

Because I am aware our heart centers can be shut off.
I choose to open my heart center by laying on my
back with my shoulder blades pressed together on the
floor. With my heart center open and my chest open- I
resume this position daily for a length of time. I send
openness in my heart center area to receive joy, peace,
love and unconditional love. I imagine this energy in
my heart center as I physically open the heart area.

Because I'm aware that trauma and pain gets stored in the pelvic area. I choose daily to lay on the floor and practice laying on my back with my legs gently open to release tension in this area. I send comfort and openness to this area by releasing all tension and pain stored here. I send openness, creativity, passion, love and care to the pelvic area with these gentle movements.

Because I look for ease in all the situations to know the path of least resistance reaps lesser unease in the body. Less is more. My focus in my thoughts is to do less and accomplish more. Our bodies at complete silence and sitting still does everything perfectly to multitask the functioning in this body and to protect this body. And these cells run this body perfectly with me doing nothing. Self-regulation and self repair is healing in this process of doing less.

Because I focus on mind body enlightenment. Exploring enlightenment with that being the goal. There is greater power of intent by living this way. There is more creativity, spontaneity and lightness of being

Because my focus is on my interbeing to evolve and
manifest. I feed my being when I'm going throughout
the day. I am... I exist... In all that exists
I am established and being. I am truthful, friendly,
blissful, and sweet. It's the realization of these
constants and one who is established in this being.

Because I choose to see what I'm grateful for. I sit
in thought to see exactly what it is. I'm grateful for
this body at minimum that it has my back and that it
protects me and that it has my best interest. I'm grateful
I am home just as I am and how I am. I'm grateful for
every cell in the body working properly for healing.
And my thankful list goes on and on and on....

Because I explore probiotics and prebiotics in foods and supplement if needed. I know how important they are in the body and linked to overall health.

Because I'm aware of the energy. I'm aware of what's
lining up with ease in my relationships and in my
life. I'm not struggling with what's not lining up.
I'm accepting what is. So the force of energy is
naturally occurring and not forced. I see what level
of energy is around me and I can see it clearly. The
universal energy lines up with matching energy.
I see it and know it and feel it. It's with ease.

Because I choose to share my healing afar now it's full circle for me. I choose to see how I released my trauma. I've captured it in the process and I'm presenting it to my best in this written form. And in my everyday life the lives that I touch I verbally share healing with ease. I am aware of people that are evolving and desiring the same. It's a natural occurring energy between people. I am vulnerable, empower and embrace the "other".

Because I'm aware of being stuck verses evolving. I'm surrounding myself with the right support people, the right resources to focus on aligning with the universe in my calling. It's fate realization taking place in the presence and manifesting in this life.

Because I am reprogramming my brain with restoration yoga. I'm releasing it from tension. I'm strengthening the right side of the brain and the left side of the brain. I do different activities for both sides of the brain. I'm very mindful of working on the brain and the importance of it. To unfreeze the brain and keep it healthy and active.

Because I explore my Ayurvedic Dosha and the things that make me thrive in that Dosha to be my best self. One of them being warmth. I implement warmth and explore the things that line up with being my best self.

Because I slowed my pace and I sat still In awareness. I allowed myself to explore my bodily vessel. How can I do right by myself? How can I reverse pain and release bodily issues? And through practicing yoga, breathing, meditation and exploring my body I decided I wanted a more in depth level. I indulged by proceeding to become a basic yoga instructor. Then proceeded with my second certification, yogafit warrior certification. I am a Certified Yogafit Warrior Teacher. I am focusing on releasing trauma in the body with movement, breathwork and meditation. The manifestation from a previous anatomy class I had taken, to exploring the active body, trauma in the body, where the trauma is stored in the body and releasing it with movement. So this is full circle for me. From being stuck feeling, unknowing, and unhealed to the healing in mind and body and releasing it now and forever. To be a freer being who can now share my story and insight amongst.

Because I focus on my equilibrium of contentment being a constant. I'm in the joyful energy state of being when I'm doing very little to nothing and also striving to maintain that state of being amongst my days.

Because I choose intention- What do I want?
I'm not looking at seeking answers. I'm asking
questions. I'm moving with questions and moving
into answers and that gives way to what I want.

Because now I have evolved my consciousness
to a state of knowingness as a whole being down
to every cell in my body. I am aware of the
connectivity of every cell in my body and that the
mind is driving the functioning in my body.

Because teaching our young ones how important the act of self love and healing actually is our lifeline. Gifting them at a young age with this insight and teaching them the act of self-love and healing. Because the true gain of the act of self-love and healing is to be able to now share beyond myself to help others of all ages.

Because I clear my chakras throughout the day. I send
positive energy to the chakras in the subtle body.
I sit in quietness and I go through the different
chakras and send open positive energy of intention,
openness, healing, joy, equanimity, peace, love
and the state of bliss (limb of yoga, Samadhi). I
do this as needed and throughout my days.

Because I do a chakra cleansing I imagine a rainbow through my central column of my body. The very areas where all the chakras are aligned in the body.

1. Red at the root chakra- I envision a positive red energy circling around the base of the spine and pelvic area. Sending it healing, creativity, joy, love, and openness to this chakra area to release any energy held up there. I send it safety, trust and vitality as it's my life force.

2. Orange at the sacral chakra- I envision a positive orange energy and bring attention to the pelvic and hips region. I send this area it openness, healing, creativity, passion and sexuality. I send it the energy to release any pent-up energy or tension.

3. Yellow at the solar plexus chakra- I imagine yellow colored energy circling the navel area. I imagine the yellow sunshine burning brightly around this area. I send it energy to manifest my intentions in the world. I send it openness and cleansing to see clearly. I send the energy to let go of hostility. I allow the energy to be free and open to my purpose and willpower and send it empowerment.

4. Green at the heart chakra- I imagine green energy circling the heart chakra and allow this to be a place of openness. I feel the unconditional openness to the heart area. I send it attention to let go of pain, to feel emotions and consciousness.

I send it energy to be filled with love, joy, harmony and peace.

5. Pale Blue at the throat chakra- I imagine and breathe in the pale blue energy as it circles the throat chakra. It is the center of expression and I send it openness. I send it the energy of the value of being and openness in the throat area. I envision speaking my truth to the people in my life I send this area positive energy of expression, knowledge and creativity.

6. Deep blue indigo at third eye chakra- I send the third eye chakra openness for insight and intuition. This is the quiet voice to the soul and it allows us to see with the eyes of the soul. We gain access to our dreams. I send openness to release all patterns of anxiety, fear, and depression that get trapped in here. I balance this chakra.

7. Golden light at the top of the head the crown chakra- I breathe in the golden light and I imagine the golden light above my crown. I send it to the openness of all of creation. I send it energy of oneness of all of creation. I send it love and the process of loving. I send it balance and openness to feel clarity and thoughts and purpose for my personal intentions and desires. This is the chakra that relates to the unbounded awareness beyond time and space.

I send this rainbow of colors and all positive energy to these chakras to rejuvenate and heal. I remind myself that I manifest my existence with every breath everyday that I'm alive.

Because I'm sending you the energy of healing,
empowerment, knowledge, love, energetic being,
lightness, enlightenment, care, compassion,
empathy, peace, bliss, openness, equanimity, calm,
stillness, passion, freedom, abundance and joy.

Namesta
-ginger

yogi

I send you healing positive energy!

Printed in the United States
by Baker & Taylor Publisher Services